How to Reach Your Full Potential: 12 Surprising Ideas to Set You Free

WILL ROSS

DEDICATION

For Kahn, Taelyn and Harlem with love and pride from Grandad.

CONTENTS

INTRODUCTION: UPGRADE YOUR LIFE

Do you ever get the impression you're not making the most of your life, that you could be accomplishing more, having more fun, feeling closer and getting along better with others? Do you spend a lot of time worrying about the future, regretting the past, or wasting the present moment?

You're not alone. Most people fail to reach their full potential. They dream of a more successful, rewarding, and joyful life for themselves. But despite their hopes and their dreams, they're held back and never attain the rich and rewarding life that could be theirs; the life that could be yours.

Why is that? Why do so many of us fail to do what we want to do with our lives? Why do we keep making the same mistakes, over and over? It seems like a mystery.

But it isn't a mystery.

Most of us fail to reach our full potential because we're held back by irrational ideas that are hardwired into every human being. Learning to recognize these ideas, and to challenge them and replace them with more uplifting ideas is the key to a successful and happy life.

What does it mean to upgrade your life and to reach your full potential? If you follow the ideas outlined in this book - ideas that were first described by Dr Albert Ellis, creator of Rational Emotive Behavior Therapy (REBT) - you'll be well on your way to living an ethical, rewarding, and joyful life, based on compassion and reason.

You'll start doing more for yourself. Hopefully, you won't ignore the interests of others, but to a large extent you'll put your own goals first. This is the only life you're likely to have, so it's important you take care of yourself and make the most of life's opportunities. When you abandon irrational ideas that hold you back, you can decide what you want to do with your life and do whatever it takes to reach your goals.

You'll choose the direction of your own life and do the things you want to do rather than going along with the herd and doing things just to please others.

You'll develop a greater tolerance for your natural human fallibility as well as the fallibility of others. You'll give yourself and others the right to be wrong, the right to be fallible, and the right to be human. You'll stop putting yourself down and condemning yourself.

You'll become more flexible and less demanding. You'll be open minded and willing to change your self-limiting beliefs and to take on new challenges you never thought possible.

You'll be more accepting of uncertainty. Instead, you'll be fascinated by the exciting possibilities that life has to offer. Instead of insisting on a guarantee that you'll be successful, you'll be willing to take a gamble and try out new adventures.

Instead of being self-absorbed, constantly fretting over your mistakes and flaws, you'll look beyond yourself and get more involved in life, committing yourself to creative pursuits that will benefit others as well as yourself. By throwing yourself into life, you'll look for ways to enhance your long-term health and happiness.

You'll develop an objective, realistic outlook that also considers the upside, and not just the downside of the challenges you face. You'll be able to assess opportunities realistically and objectively, and won't be deterred by irrational beliefs that have held you back in the past.

You'll begin to see life as an adventure. Without being foolhardy, you'll take risks and go after the things you want, even though you fully accept the possibility that you could fail. By taking chances and risking failure, you'll put yourself in a position to reach your goals.

You'll put your focus on your long-term happiness. Instead of taking the quick, easy route that leads to long-term frustration and disappointment, you'll be willing to put up with some short-term discomfort and inconvenience in order to satisfy your long-term ambitions.

You'll be more accepting of the fact that there's no heaven on earth and you're unlikely to get everything you want, or avoid all discomfort and pain. You'll push yourself to pursue what's possible - a joyful, meaningful existence - without chasing after a non-existent utopia.

You'll stop blaming life or other people for your woes, and take responsibility for the way you feel and the things you do. Instead of being a victim, you'll think for yourself while proactively and decisively choosing how to feel and what to do.

You'll accept yourself warts and all. Instead of putting yourself down, you'll focus on enjoying life rather than trying to prove yourself. You'll show yourself the same compassion you would to any other human being struggling with the hassles of day-to-day existence. You'll develop a growing confidence in the idea that although you're not perfect, you are not a second-rate human being.

You'll stop isolating yourself and join with others to get involved in community projects that help you to make your community a better place in which to live, creating the kind of world in which you can thrive.

So let's get started on your journey to a new rewarding and fulfilling life by exploring Idea #1: You don't need love and approval.

***

IDEA #1: YOU DON'T NEED LOVE AND APPROVAL

Tom is lonely. He desperately wants a girlfriend. In many respects, he leads a happy and successful life: he has a good job with good pay; he's popular with his workmates and has a number of close friends outside of work; he takes care of his health and body by eating well and exercising regularly; and he has a good singing voice that others envy. But he has no love life. He knows a few women he'd like to date but he's afraid of rejection so he avoids asking them out. He worries that his friends will look down on him when they find out the women have turned him down. In his own mind, Tom believes other people must like and respect him so he avoids doing anything that might bring about disapproval or rejection. Tom's need for approval affects his life in other ways: he often goes out of his way to make sure people are happy, frequently going along with what they want to do rather than doing what he wants. If he disagrees with someone, he keeps his mouth shut so as not to antagonize them and earn their scorn. Later, he berates himself for being so cowardly.

Most people want to be liked. Few of us enjoy getting into an argument, or being criticized or rejected. Having the approval of others makes it easier to get a good job, gain a promotion, make friends, and to find a spouse or lover. But many people turn the desire for approval into a need. They're convinced that they *must*

5

make a good impression and have everyone's approval and they *must* never be disliked, criticized, or rejected.

The idea that you *must* have others' approval is irrational - unhelpful, illogical, and unrealistic - for several reasons.

If you think about it carefully, you'll agree that it's impossible to be liked by everyone. Even some of the most popular people in history (e.g., Mother Teresa, Martin Luther King, Mahatma Gandhi, the Beatles, Jesus Christ, et cetera) were not universally liked or loved. They had their detractors. No matter how popular you are, no matter how many friends you have, no matter how much you go out of your way to be liked, there will always be some people who don't like you, who are not impressed by you, and who will criticize and reject you.

One of the reasons it's impossible to have universal approval is that different people have different tastes. Some people may be impressed by your new hairstyle, or your ability to play classical piano, but other people might be turned off completely by it. Therefore no matter what you do, some people will admire and respect you, but others will have the completely opposite opinion. It's not your fault. It's just human nature.

But suppose you could make yourself universally popular and get everyone to like you, you could never be certain that they would like you *enough*, or that they will always like you. You may have their approval today, but can you count on having it tomorrow?

Trying to get people to like you takes time and effort. The more people you to try to please, the more time and effort you'll have to put into your Endeavour. By the time you finish pleasing everyone, you won't have enough time or energy left over to do the things you want to do.

If you demand others' approval and convince yourself you need it, like Tom, you'll always be doing what others want you to do, instead of doing what you want to do with your time and your life.

Your life will no longer be your own; you'll have given it away to everyone else.

If you can get others to like you by going along with what they want rather than doing what you want, you will, in effect, have stopped being you. You'll be someone who pretends to enjoy certain activities when in fact you don't. You'll be nothing more than a puppet manipulated by the desires of others. And if others admire you - because you seem like an agreeable person - it won't be you they admire: It'll be the person you're pretending to be.

If you try too hard to gain the approval of others, they'll soon tire of you. They'll get sick of the way you constantly fawn over them and kowtow to them. Eventually, they'll lose all respect for you; they'll take advantage of you and treat you like a doormat. Through your alleged need for approval, through your actions, through your sycophancy, you'll have lost their approval and gained the exact opposite of what you were trying to achieve.

Having the respect, admiration, and approval of others doesn't necessarily mean you'll feel that way about yourself. If you disapprove of yourself, no matter how much others admire you, you'll feel miserable. Rather than trying to impress others, you'll get greater benefit from accepting yourself, no matter what others think of you.

It's not pleasant when other people don't like you, when they criticize and reject you, but it's not the end of the world; it's not fatal. There's no evidence that you *must* make a good impression on others, no evidence that you *need* respect and approval. There's no harm in trying to be popular, liked, and respected, but it's best not to try too hard. You'll no doubt find it helpful and satisfying to have the approval of others, but it's self-defeating when you turn the desire for approval into an absolute need.

You'll find life is far more satisfying if you pay less attention to how much approval you're receiving, and instead, focus on showing your approval and appreciation for others. As a bonus, you'll probably find the more attention and gratitude you show to others, the more you'll get from them.

Like Tom, you'll find your life far more satisfying if you give up your *need* for approval and be willing to risk rejection and disapproval to get what you want.

Key Point: Having the approval of others has its benefits but you don't need it. You don't have to make a good impression on everyone you meet.

***

IDEA #2: YOU DON'T HAVE TO BE SUCCESSFUL

Claire dreams of being a writer. She has an idea for a novel but she puts off writing it because she's afraid it won't be good enough. In her mind, if her novel isn't a great bestseller then there's no point writing it. For Claire, failure isn't an option. Claire believes that if her novel was unsuccessful, her friends and family would find out and she'd be utterly humiliated. Her failed novel would prove to the world that she was a failure.

Wayne hates to fail at anything. No matter what he's doing, whether it's at work, at home, or playing his favorite sport of tennis, he loves to succeed, he loves to win. He doesn't enjoy activities where he can't succeed or where he can't do things as well as others. If he can, he'll avoid doing them at all. His friends have tried encouraging him to try other sports, but he refuses because he's afraid he'll get beaten by better, more experienced players. Wayne is afraid to make errors, and often gets angry with himself whenever he makes a mistake. He tells himself that he must be competent at everything he does, and if he's not competent then he sees himself as an inferior human being.

Being competent and successful has many advantages. It can save you time and money. Mistakes are inconvenient; they mean you'll often have to repeat your work or learn to live with substandard results. When you succeed at something - at work, at home, or at play - you get a sense of achievement. For many reasons, it's worth your while to strive for success and competence in a variety of areas of your life. But the convenience and sense of achievement that comes with being successful are no reason to turn a desire for success into a *need* for success.

The idea that you *must* be thoroughly competent, adequate, and achieving in all possible respects has several significant flaws.

You can't be good at everything. Nobody can. You may be a great tennis player, but that doesn't mean you'll be a brilliant guitarist. Few get to be outstanding in any chosen area - there are only a handful of truly great physicists, for example - but even fewer get to exceed in more than one area. Most of us aren't outstandingly good at even one thing, let alone everything. We are, after all, mere mortals.

Being successful has its rewards so it's worth striving for. But if you try too hard to succeed - especially if you try to succeed at everything - you'll create unnecessary stress for yourself. By all means, retain your desire to succeed, but stubbornly refuse to *insist* on success, refuse to absolutely *need* success.

Frequently, by focusing on success, you lose sight of the process involved to be successful. As a result, you end up making more mistakes than if you were just to focus on the process rather than the ultimate outcome. Worse, focusing on the outcome robs you of the enjoyment of the process. If you're overly determined to beat your golfing partner, you'll make yourself upset whenever you play a poor shot, and you won't enjoy the game. Surely enjoying the game while you play it is more important than actually winning it.

Success - for example, when you apply for a job - often means competing against others. If you convince yourself that you *must* be successful , that you *must* get the job, you pay too much attention to what your competitors can do and lose sight of your own strengths and weaknesses. In the end, you can't control what other people do, or how well they can do it. If you're determined to succeed, you'll be competing against something over which you have no control.

No matter how much you try, there will be some things you'll never succeed at because you have little or no control over your own abilities. Much of what we can and can't do is determined by our genetic make-up. For example, you can't be a successful musician if you were born tone deaf. Nor will you succeed as professional basketballer if you're only 5 feet tall.

Being successful won't make you a better person. Your true, intrinsic worth comes from being alive. Your ability to participate in life is what you gives your life worth and meaning. Nothing else matters, least of all your ability to sink a 9-yard putt.

Working hard to be successful usually takes time and effort, especially at tasks that don't come naturally to you. If you're too busy trying to be successful at everything, you'll fall behind in your work, and won't have time left over for doing the things you enjoy.

If you're convinced that you *must* be successful and competent at everything you do, you'll be afraid to try new tasks. You'll find yourself doing the same things over and over. Your life will become boring because you'll only do the things you know you can succeed at, and you'll never get to try new experiences.

The best way to learn how to do something is to just do it. The way to succeed is to practice, practice, practice and to learn from your mistakes. Mistakes and failure are not awful; they're a normal part of learning. Human beings fail and make mistakes all the time. If you make a mistake, it doesn't make you worthless - it proves that you're a normal human being.

Key Point: Success and competence have their rewards but you don't *have* to be competent and you don't *have* to be successful.

***

IDEA #3: NOBODY HAS TO DO WHAT YOU WANT THEM TO DO

Jonathan threw the remote control at his television set. He was enraged because he'd just heard on the news that another criminal had gotten away with a light sentence. Jonathan believes that people who do wrong deserve to be severely punished, and too many wrongdoers escape the punishment they deserve. Jonathan has a clear sense of what's right and what's wrong. He believes that everyone must always do the right thing. Those who do wrong deserve to be called-out, blamed, and condemned. In Jonathan's mind, if someone does something bad, it means they are a bad person, and the fear of punishment will help them to overcome their basic evil nature, and become good citizens. Jonathan treats his friends and family the same way; he is quick to condemn them and he flies into a rage when they don't do what he believes they should. He seldom gives anyone a second chance.

It's not unreasonable to feel annoyed when you're frustrated by events or by other people, when you don't get what you want. But getting angry is a completely different kettle of fish. When you're annoyed, you're motivated to make changes and to act assertively to get what you want. But when you're angry, you feel far worse than you need to; your anger stays with you long after the event; it interferes with other areas of your life and with your relationships with others; and it makes it harder for you make positive changes in your life.

We all want people to behave in certain ways, we want them to do what we believe is right, and to act in socially-appropriate ways. Wanting "correct" behavior from others is one thing. Demanding that they do what is "right," is quite another thing. There's no reason why people *must* do what we want them to do, and the practice of blaming, condemning, and brutally punishing others for their misdeeds is counter-productive.

The idea that some people are evil and that they *must* be blamed and punished for their wrongdoing is faulty for a variety of reasons.

Nobody is perfect. We all make mistakes and, from time to time, we act in ways we later regret. The truth is we don't have total control over all our actions. We make mistakes and treat others badly because (1) we don't know any better, it is not our fault that no one has taught us the correct way to behave; (2) for one reason or another we lack the ability to do the right thing; or (3) we are naturally fallible human beings, highly capable of making mistakes and doing the wrong thing. To expect others to always do the right thing is to expect the impossible.

If you blame and punish someone for making a mistake because he doesn't know any better, your actions won't make him any smarter or more competent. Similarly, condemning and punishing someone for a mistake they made while they were physically or mentally unable to do differently won't necessarily help him to do better next time. And finally, abusing and punishing someone for a mistake they make because they are a natural, fallible human being - just like you and me - won't make them any less fallible.

Think how many things you do each day. Many of your actions are conscious and deliberate, but far more are unconscious; much of the time you're totally unaware of what you're doing. Some of the things you do are "bad," some are "good," and some are neither "good" nor "bad." The "bad" things you do don't make you a "bad person;" and the "good" things you do don't make you a "good person." You are, like everyone else who has ever lived, a person who does some "good" and some "bad" deeds. That's what it means to be human. No one is either completely good nor completely bad.

If you tell someone she is a "bad person," she may foolishly agree with you and the idea that she's a "bad person" will become an integral part of her self-image. Then, because she sees herself as a completely "bad person," she'll do more "bad" things, because that's what "bad people" do. She'll try to live up to - or more correctly, live down to - the label.

When you punish others for their mistakes, when you make them suffer, instead of trying to improve their behavior, they may instead seek revenge and act even worse in the future.

Blaming and condemning people for their mistakes carries a high emotional cost. When you blame yourself for your mistakes, you become fearful and depressed. When you blame and punish others for their mistakes, you become angry and bigoted. Then, to make matters worse, you blame and condemn yourself for your unhealthy, unhelpful emotions. The more you blame and condemn, the more upset you become; and the more upset you become, the more reason you have to blame and condemn yourself. Once you get on this not-so-merry-go-round, it's exceedingly difficult to get off.

From time to time, you'll be on the receiving end of someone else's blaming and condemning. They may verbally abuse you and try to punish you. When this happens, ask yourself if you really did anything wrong. If you did do something wrong, apologies and try not to do it again. If, on the other hand, you didn't do anything wrong, you can remind yourself that the other person is mistaken and that they can't help making mistakes. There's no reason to blame yourself for the other person's mistake, nor is there any reason to condemn them for their mistake. They are, after all, human.

There will always be people who act in socially inappropriate ways. But it's not the end of the world when others behave badly, selfishly, or unfairly. Making yourself upset over their poor behavior won't do anything to change it. If you can teach them to behave better, then do so. But if you can't teach them to do better next time, then you might as well learn to live with their mistakes and remind yourself that there's no law of the universe compelling people to act appropriately; their behavior is unfortunate but it won't stop the earth from spinning.

Most importantly, give yourself permission to make mistakes. You're human, and making mistakes is what humans were born to do. By all means, try to avoid mistakes and treat others fairly when you can, but don't give yourself a hard time when you fail to live up to your standards. Remember, there are no guarantees in life, and you can't guarantee that you'll always act competently and appropriately.

Key Point: It's natural to want others to do the right thing but nobody has to do what you want them to do, and blaming and punishing others for their misdeeds serves little purpose.

***

IDEA #4: IT'S NOT THE END OF THE WORLD IF YOU DON'T GET YOUR WAY

Jill has never considered the possibility of philosophically accepting her disappointments and taking them in her stride. She believes that disappointments shouldn't happen, and that things very often should be different from the way they are. Jill sees every disappointment and frustration as a catastrophe. She makes herself disturbed over situations she doesn't like and believes that her frustrations are the cause of her emotional turmoil. She can't ignore things she finds annoying, and insists on getting what she wants. She obsesses over situations that aren't to her liking. She thinks it's natural to be upset over frustrations and believes that people are obviously unhappy when they have challenges and problems to overcome.

Every day we run into events that are not to our liking. It's ironic that in our pursuit of happiness, frustrations and disappointments are a natural part of life. When you're goals are thwarted, it's natural to feel unhappy. It makes no sense, and is of little value, to be delighted when you don't get what you want. On the other hand, it makes no sense, and is of little value, to make mountains out of molehills. Jumping up and down, screaming blue bloody murder, doesn't solve your problems, it merely serves to make you miserable.

The idea that it is *terrible* and *catastrophic* when things are not the way you want them to be is irrational on a number of fronts.

If you had a magic wand, you could make the world a better place, more to your liking. But you don't have a magic wand. The universe doesn't conform to your dictates. There's no reason why things *must* be the way you want them to be, no matter how unfair they are now. Unfortunate events and inconveniences happen in this world. That's just the way it is. Of course, that doesn't mean you have to be thrilled when unfortunate events occur. But getting upset won't solve your problems, it won't make them go away, it won't improve matters.

When you make mountains out of molehills, when you tell yourself that an unfortunate situation is nothing short of a disaster, you make yourself upset and miserable. The more upset you get, the less effective you'll be at solving your problems and changing the things you don't like.

Have you ever witnessed a two-year-old in a supermarket, lying on the floor, screaming and kicking because his mother won't buy him the candy he wants? Just because two-year-olds have temper tantrums when they don't get they want, it doesn't mean you have to have one when you don't get what you want. While the temper tantrum may be an effective strategy for the two-year-old, it's rarely effective for adults. If you can change things you don't like, then go ahead and change them. Go after the things you want. But when you can't get your own way, you'll save yourself much time and effort if you learn to live with the disappointment without crying like a baby.

Many people, like Jill, believe that their frustrations and disappointments are the cause of their emotional turmoil. This belief is, however, false. It's not the frustration and the disappointment that makes you upset - it's your rigid and extreme view of the disappointment that makes you miserable. The more you tell yourself you *should* have what you want and that it's *awful* when you don't get what you want, the more upset you'll be. But if you recognize that the world does not operate according to your commandments, and that it's not a catastrophe when you don't get what you want, you'll be able to approach your problems in a calm, courageous, and compassionate manner.

When things are not to your liking, and you can't change them, you can tell yourself, "I wish they were different, but it's not the end of the world, and it won't kill me if I have to keep putting up with them." Then try to learn from them, accept them as challenges, and see if there's some way you can use them in your life. If that doesn't work, do your best to ignore them and do something else you enjoy doing.

Key Point: It's disappointing when you don't get what you want but it's not the end of the world.

***

IDEA #5: YOU FEEL THE WAY YOU THINK

Terence finds it impossible to be happy unless everything is going smoothly for him. When he's miserable, he tends to sit around and do nothing, letting his problems mount and not pursuing his goals. He believes it's only natural for him to get upset when things go wrong. He claims he can't help the way he feels, that bad situations make people feel bad, and there's nothing you can do about feeling upset. He sees no point in trying to change his bad feelings. Whenever Terence is in a bad mood he believes he'll just have to wait until the mood goes away on its own. He also believes that the more problems someone has, the less happy they'll be, and people who are upset usually have a good reason for it.

The idea that the events in our lives cause our emotional reaction to those events seems, at first blush, to make sense. After all, when good things happen to us, we usually feel good, and when bad things happen to us, we usually feel bad.

But if you think about it carefully, you'll soon see that not everybody reacts the same to similar situations. For example, some people are devastated when they fail at an exam; some people are disappointed by the failure but hardly devastated; while others couldn't care less. If our emotions were caused by events, then we would all react exactly the same to similar events. The fact that we

19

have different reactions clearly indicates that something else is at work.

The first-century philosopher, Epictetus, gave us the answer: "People are not upset by events, but by the view they take of them." In other words, it's not your circumstances that cause your emotional reactions. Your emotional reactions are the result of what you tell yourself about the things that happen. In short, your thoughts, beliefs, and attitudes cause your feelings and your actions. Throughout your life, the situations you find yourself in will trigger thoughts and beliefs that produce your emotional and behavioral reactions.

The idea that your unhappiness is caused by your circumstances and that you have little or no ability to control your emotions is clearly false.

It's impossible for someone to harm you unless they beat you up or rob you, or otherwise physically harm you. They can hurt you physically, but they can't hurt you emotionally. For example, if someone insults you, it's not *their* words that upset you - it's *your* words. You make yourself upset either by agreeing with their insult or by choosing to take offence at it. You might believe that the other person is harming you, but the real cause of the pain is what you're telling yourself about the insult.

It's nonsense for you to say, "It hurts me when people are unfair," or "I can't stand it when things go wrong." Whatever "it" is, "it" can't hurt you. The only thing that can hurt you is your beliefs. The reality is that you upset yourself by believing that it's *awful* when people are unfair or when things go wrong, and that the world *should* be a better place where people are fair and things always go right.

It's a common belief that human happiness is externally caused. Most people believe they can't control their feelings. But they're wrong! Although it's not easy to change the way you feel, it's not impossible. When you feel upset - depressed, anxious, or enraged -

look for your irrational beliefs (your *musts*, your *shoulds*, your *awfuls*, and your *I can't stand its*) and change them to more flexible, less extreme evaluations.

Albert Ellis created the ABC model to show how demands lead to dysfunctional emotions. Here's how it works:

A. Something happens.

B. You make a demand about the situation.

C. You have an emotional reaction to the demand.

Here's an example that shows the ABC model in action.

Something happens, (for example, your boss fires you for something that wasn't your fault) and you react (for example, you get angry). Remember that losing your job doesn't cause the anger. It's your demands about losing your job that make you angry. In simple, ABC terms we have the following:

A. Something happens (in this case, getting fired unfairly)

B. Belief or demand (about the job loss)

C. Reaction as a result of the demand (anger)

It looks like this:

A. I was fired unfairly for something that wasn't my fault.

B. My boss *should* not have fired me; she had *no right* to do that. Bosses *should* always give their employees a fair deal.

C. I feel angry.

If, instead of demanding that your boss not fire you, you'd changed your demand to a preference, you'd have felt annoyed rather than angry. Hence:

A. I was fired unfairly for something that wasn't my fault.

B. It's unfair that my boss fired me for something that wasn't my fault and I wish she had kept me on. But there's no reason why bosses must always act fairly. They're human and prone to making mistakes, just like the rest of us.

C. I feel annoyed.

The ABC model shows that **A** (what happens) does not cause **B** (your feelings). It' **B** (your demands) that cause **C**. It's not your being fired that made you angry; it's your *demand* that your boss treat you fairly and *must* not fire you.

Key Point: Things, people, and circumstances don't upset you; you upset yourself. You feel the way you think.

***

IDEA #6: WORRYING WON'T HELP

Hayley often feels anxious. Because she worries so much about unexpected dangers and future events, she finds it difficult to concentrate and to enjoy the pleasure of the present moment. Hayley spends a lot of time and energy thinking about things that could go wrong, and planning what she'll do if disaster strikes. She ruminates over her problems, seemingly unable to get them off her mind. She's paralyzed by her fear, unwilling to take chances in case things turn out badly and others think less of her. Her life has become a fear-filled rut where she refuses to step outside her comfort zone. Although bright and talented, she has failed to do much with her life.

Fear and worry come in two flavors: (1) fear that your safety and comfort will be threatened, and (2) fear that your self-image will be threatened.

Fear of discomfort comes from such thoughts as "I must get what I want and must not be inconvenienced or troubled." "My life must be safe, secure, and predictable." "I must avoid difficult situations and prepare for anything that might go wrong."

You may experience self-image fear when your view of yourself or your personal worth is threatened by failing at an important task and having others look down on you. It's not so much the failure or the disapproval that creates the fear as the belief that you *must* not fail and you *must* not lose the approval of others, otherwise you're *no good* and *worthless*, that creates self-image anxiety.

Fear once served a useful purpose for our ancient ancestors: it made them alert and prepared their muscles to fight or run away from real dangers. But today, fear is more of a handicap than a helper: it prevents us from taking reasonable risks to go after the things we want. Many people avoid doing what they want with their lives because they're terrified of failure and believe they must avoid it at all costs.

The idea that you *must* avoid failure and *must* dwell on dangers and pitfalls is irrational for several reasons.

Most of our fears are for things that aren't really dangerous, e.g., failing an exam or being rejected by a potential lover. If you're confronted by something that seems dangerous, ask yourself if it poses a genuine threat to your body. If it does, then by all means avoid it. Whether it's a real danger or an imagined one, worrying about it won't help you. In fact, you'll probably deal with it less effectively if you're consumed by worry and fear.

Worrying about possible failures and rejection won't make it more likely you'll succeed in your reaching your goals. In fact, it'll often make it more likely you'll fail because instead of focusing on doing what's necessary to succeed, your thoughts and energy are focused on the possibility of calamity striking.

People who worry about failure expect to fail more frequently than people who don't worry about it. This sets up a vicious cycle: First they worry about failure, then they expect to fail, which only makes them worry more about failing.

Rejection and failure are a natural part of life: they happen to all of us, from time to time. Worrying about them won't rid them from your life. Instead, it'll make life less enjoyable. You'll have two problems for the price of one: (1) living with occasional failure and rejection, and (2) spending many unnecessarily unhappy years worrying about failure and rejection.

Failure and rejection aren't pleasant but they're not the end of the world, you'll survive them. The more time you spend worrying about them, the worse you'll come to view them. And the worse you view them, the more you'll obsess over the likelihood of them occurring.

Rather than avoiding the things you fear (such as asking someone out on a date or applying for a promotion), you'd be much better off going out of your way to do them. In time, with repeated practice, you'll soon see there is no reason to be afraid of them.

Key Point: When you pursue your goals you'll sometimes fail or lose the respect of others, but there's no reason to let that possibility prevent you from going after what you want in life; dwelling on the prospect of failure and rejection won't make your life any easier, it'll only make it less pleasant.

***

IDEA #7: YOU'LL ACHIEVE MORE BY DOING THE WORST FIRST

Tanner believes an easy life is a good life. He finds it practically impossible to motivate himself to do unpleasant chores. He hates having responsibilities, and avoids facing up to his problems. Even when something is important, if it's unpleasant to deal with, he'll avoid doing it for as long as he can get away with it. Procrastination seems to be his middle name, and if he doesn't want to do something then he leaves it until the last possible minute. Tanner believes life is too short to spend doing unpleasant tasks.

By definition, if a task is unpleasant then we don't want to do it. But wishing we didn't have to do it won't make it go away, nor will it make it any more pleasant when we ultimately face up to it. Many of us are just like Tanner: we may not be able to avoid facing up to a task, but we'll keep the task waiting for as long as we possibly can before we get around to tackling it.

The idea that it's easier to avoid challenges and responsibilities than it is to face up to them is self-defeating for several reasons.

When you avoid an unpleasant or difficult task, you may get a pleasant sense of relief. But the relief is only temporary. While you

26

might feel better at the exact moment of avoidance, you'll later regret your decision and wish you'd faced up to the task when you had the opportunity. For example, you might avoid asking for a pay rise and feel better immediately because you avoided the risk of failure and rejection. But later, you'll kick yourself for being so cowardly and missing out on the opportunity for more money.

Suppose you have to write a report for work but you tell yourself that the task of writing is so awful that you must avoid it. You spend hours planning for ways to avoid writing the report, and then more hours thinking of an excuse for not doing it. The longer you put off writing the report, the longer you spend worrying about. Instead of just getting it over and done with, you prolong your unhappiness.

The more practice you have doing something, the easier it becomes. But if you avoid doing difficult tasks, you'll never get the practice you need to make the job easier. The difficult task will remain difficult, and you'll never get the confidence to do it.

Trying out new tasks makes our life and exciting adventure. If you spend your life sitting around doing nothing except very easy tasks, you'll soon become bored. But if you try new experiences and work at doing things that are quite difficult, you'll gain a sense of achievement, and your life will be much happier and more rewarding.

Sometimes a task is unnecessary. If it is unnecessary and unpleasant, then it makes sense to avoid it. But if a task is going to make your life easier or more enjoyable in the long run, then the sooner you do it, the better.

Some people think they are born lazy. But that's a false belief. You were not born lazy. Laziness is nothing more than a bad habit of telling yourself things about work which aren't true. You can overcome your "laziness" by telling yourself (1) work isn't all that bad, (2) there is no reason why you must avoid unpleasant tasks, and (3) the sooner you get an unpleasant task done the better.

There's no point doing unnecessary tasks for the mere sake of just doing them. But if a job is necessary or it'll make your life easier in the long run, then (1) remember that the sooner you get the job done the better, (2) decide when you are going to do the job, (3) make sure you do it at the time you've decided to do it, (4) if it's a big job, do little bits at a time, and (5) give yourself a reward after you complete each part of the job.

The longer you put off facing a task, the longer you'll have to worry about it. If a task takes, say, an hour to complete, and you spend six hours worrying about it and finding ways to avoid it, the whole thing will have given you a total of seven hours of misery. But if you did the task immediately, you could avoid six hours of misery, and only have the task to face. Multiply this by all the times you procrastinate, and you'll soon see that it's not worth the effort.

You only have one life, and it's for living. If you're tired, then by all means take a rest. But don't spend your entire life resting. Do as much as you can with your life. Try things that might be difficult or unpleasant first, keep doing them until you get good at them and find you enjoy doing them.

If you have a number of jobs or chores to do on any given day, do the worst one first. Ask yourself, "Which of these tasks would I like not to have to do?" Whichever task is the one you least want to do, do that one first. Get it out of the way. If, on the other hand, you leave the dreaded task till last knowing you'll have to face it eventually, it will take away much of the pleasure you get from the other, more enjoyable tasks.

Key Point: It's easier to tackle difficult or unpleasant tasks as soon as possible than it is to keep putting them off.

***

IDEA #8: EMBRACE YOUR INDEPENDENCE

Misty lacks the confidence to do very much on her own and frequently calls on others for help and advice. Rather than learning new skills, she prefers to let others do things for her, even if it means paying them or having to wait for the job to be done. Whenever she has an important decision to make, she asks a friend or family member to make the decision for her. She depends on them greatly. Misty hates the idea of standing on her own two feet; she believes she couldn't do it on her own and that she needs a source of strength outside herself to rely on. She doesn't want to take control of her life; she'd rather let others take charge and direct her.

Some people don't like to ask for help when they need it, usually because they're afraid of rejection and disapproval. So being able to ask for help is a good thing. But many people, like Misty, take the opposite extreme and become overly reliant on others. They believe they need someone stronger and more competent than themselves to make their decisions and to do things for them. By being so overly reliant on others, they sacrifice their freedom as well as their independence.

The idea that you can't be independent and need to rely on someone who is smarter or stronger than you prevents you from reaching your full potential for several reasons.

Obviously, you can't do everything for yourself. From time to time, you'll need to call on others to fix your car, treat your illnesses, or build your house, et cetera. But the more you can do for yourself the better. Being independent gives you more control over your life. If you become too dependent on others, you'll lose control of your life while allowing others to make your choices and do your thinking. Cooperating with others often leads to great things, but being overly depending on others leads to an unfulfilled life.

Getting others to do things for you comes with a price. It could be a financial cost, or it could be a practical cost. In order to get their help, you may have to give something back in return, including your autonomy. You may have to do what they want instead of doing what you want. You'll live with the fear that if you don't do what they want, they won't be there for you next time you ask for their help. In effect, you'll have given up your freedom and become their slave.

The more you rely on others, the less chance you have to add to your skill set and gain competency. As a result, you'll have less confidence in your ability to carry out tasks. The less skilled you are, the less confident you'll feel, and the more you'll come to depend on others. It will create a vicious circle where (1) you rely on others to do things for you, (2) you lose confidence in yourself, so (3) you rely even more on others to do things for you.

If you rely on others to make you feel safe and secure, you'll actually become less safe and secure because you're less able to look after yourself and take care of your own safety and security.

Existence isn't stable. The people you rely on might one day move to another city or they might die. Or they may just get sick of being at your beck and call. You can't be certain the person you rely on will always be around. Therefore, the less you rely on others and the more you can rely on yourself, the better equipped you'll be to cope with change.

This is your life. You have your own goals and dreams. You're the only person who knows what you really want in life. The more you rely on others to provide you with what you want, the less sure you can be that you'll get it. The more you can count on yourself, the greater chance you have of getting exactly what you want out of life.

You don't have to have what you want in life. If you try to get something you want and fail, it's not the end of the world. You can always try again, and keep practicing until you develop the necessary skills to get what you want out of life.

Key Point: From time to time you may need to rely on others to help you with certain projects, but the more you can do for yourself, the more independent you can be, the easier you'll find it to reach your goals and find fulfillment.

***

IDEA #9: YOU'RE PAST YOUR PAST

Jerome doesn't have a very high opinion of himself. He has always considered himself inferior to others and unworthy. Jerome blames his parents for his lack of confidence and low self-esteem. As a child, they were always criticizing him and finding fault with everything he did, frequently comparing him unfavorably to his younger brother. Now, in his 30s, he has taken on his parent's role and become his own harshest critic, constantly putting himself down for his imperfections. He believes he can't overcome the influences of the past and sees himself as nothing but a flawed individual, a failure. He doesn't like the negative view he has of himself and would like to see himself in a more positive light but he says, "That's just the way I am. I've always seen myself this way. A zebra can't change its stripes and I can't suddenly change the way I see myself. My parents made me this way and there's nothing I can do about it."

To some degree, you were shaped by your early childhood experiences. You learned to see yourself, others, and the world in general in a certain way. But the way you see the world is not set in concrete. Just because you believed something in your childhood, doesn't mean you have to believe it today. You don't have to be a slave to your personal history. You can overcome the influences of the past, see yourself in a different light, and take on new challenges.

The idea that your past history, especially your childhood, has set your life on an unalterable path so that you can't change and must stay the same as you've always been is pure nonsense. It serves as an unnecessary millstone around your neck, preventing you from reaching your full potential.

Some of the foolish ideas you learned as a child, such as the idea that you must win others' approval and must not fail at important tasks, remain with you today because you keep repeating them to yourself. If you would stop for a minute and listen to your inner dialogue, you will easily see that these ideas are no longer applicable, and can be safely discarded.

Just because people had a big effect on your life when you are younger doesn't mean they must always have that effect. For example, taking direction from authority figures, such as parents and teachers, probably served you well as a child. But you're no longer a child, so you don't need to rely on others to make decisions for you now. You can decide to yourself what you want out of life and can - mostly - do whatever you please.

When you were a child, your parents or teachers may have cruelly told you you were stupid and useless. Because you were young and impressionable, you believed them. But you don't have to continue believing such nonsense. You can see yourself in a more compassionate light, recognizing that like everyone else on the planet, you will, from time to time, make mistakes and fail on important tasks. But that doesn't make you stupid and useless. It merely proves that you're a normal, fallible human being, just like the rest of us.

Some solutions and tactics work quite well for 2-year-olds. For example, lying on the supermarket floor, crying and screaming, may encourage the child's mother to buy him the candy he wants. But those tactics don't work quite so well for adults. Most problems have several solutions, but the more you continue to rely on childish solutions, the less likely it is you'll be able to find better, more adult solutions to your problems.

If you convince yourself that you can't change, the less likely you'll be to try new experiences. For example, if as a teenager you didn't enjoy foreign cuisine, you may be unwilling to try it later in life. Whereas if you did try it, you may find that you actually enjoy it. Similarly, if you're willing to untether yourself from the past, you might find you enjoy playing different sports, or attempting to play a new musical instrument, or meeting new people.

Throughout your life, you'll run into a variety of different problems. If you make the effort, you can usually find solutions to the problems you have today. But blaming your problems on your childhood is just a poor excuse for not trying to solve your present problems.

Similarly, you'll run into a variety of different opportunities. But if you see yourself as fixed and immutable, you may shy away from the opportunities life presents to you.

As a child, you learned some foolish, self-defeating ideas, and developed habits that no longer serve you well. Changing those ideas and habits isn't always easy, but nor is it impossible. You can, with work and practice, change the way you talk to yourself and break the habits of the past.

Key Point: You might not be able to change yourself entirely in a single day, but you can, if you work persistently and steadily, radically change yourself over time so you can reach your goals and live the kind of life you want to lead.

***

IDEA #10: THERE'S NO USE CRYING OVER SOMEONE ELSE'S SPILLED MILK

Sharon likes to take charge of other people's lives. She's quick to offer advice whenever her friends have a problem and insists on helping them do what she regards as the right thing. She often makes recommendations to her friends about who they should or shouldn't date, what job they should or shouldn't take, et cetera. She believes it would be heartless not to get upset when other people have a problem and that getting upset is a good way to help them. She spends a lot of time worrying about other people's problems, often neglecting her own problems. When they do something that Sharon believes is mistaken, she feels angry and sees it as her responsibility to point them in the right direction and to help them fix the error.

Part of being a good friend is being willing and able to help your friends when they have problems or when they ask for your advice. But many people, like Sharon, go overboard and become overly interfering. They make martyrs of themselves becoming overly upset whenever someone else has a problem. They become like overprotective mother hens, hovering over their friends as a hen would over her chicks, taking care of every little problem, offering advice when none is asked for, and making sure their friends and family stay out of trouble.

Subscribing to the idea that you should be upset over other people's problems will, for a number of reasons, prevent you from reaching your full potential.

You have your own life to lead. Other people's problems usually have nothing to do with you. Although empathy is a natural and often helpful part of the human condition, there's no reason why you must make yourself feel upset and become involved every time someone you care about has a problem.

We all see the world differently. The people you care about will often make choices and do things you disagree with. But that doesn't make them criminals or subhuman. You don't have to take charge and insist that they take another direction. If you get angry over their choices and actions, you won't help yourself, and you certainly won't help them. All you'll do is contribute to your own misery.

Sometimes, other people's behavior will affect you. They may be unfair or rude towards you. But again, getting upset won't change things. It won't help you, and it won't help them. Your anger or your sense of hurt over other people's behavior towards you is not a result of their behavior; it is a result of your belief that other people *must* act fairly and politely towards you.

If you've ever tried to change yourself - say, by eating less, or taking up exercise, or giving up procrastination, et cetera - you may have noticed that it's not easy. Although it's not easy to change yourself, it is possible with hard work and persistence. You do have some power to change yourself, but you have very little - if any - power to change others. Getting upset will not give you any more power to change others. In fact, your emotional overreaction to other people's behavior will frequently reduce your influence over them. Indeed, some people may enjoy seeing you upset and, instead of changing, they may increase the behavior you dislike in an attempt to upset you more.

You may be able to motivate some people to change by getting angry or upset with them. But is it worth it? Anger is an extremely unpleasant emotion to experience. Surely there are better, less painful ways to change people than by making yourself feel bad. For instance, you may find that you can be just as effective in changing others by calmly, yet assertively, letting them know how their actions impact you, and politely but forcefully asking them to change.

Being happy and reaching your full potential often involves changing the way you think, and changing the things you do. If you spend the bulk of your time trying to change others, you won't have time left over to change yourself. If you really want to reach your full potential, then getting upset over other people's problems is not the way to do it. In fact, interfering in other people's problems is often a copout, an excuse for not changing your thinking and behavior or solving your own problems.

Key Point: There's no reason why you must get upset over other people's problems and behaviors. In fact, interfering in other people's lives will frequently prevent you from reaching your full potential.

***

IDEA #11: CLOSE ENOUGH IS GOOD ENOUGH

Kenny recently graduated from college and now has a dilemma: he can't decide whether to enroll in grad school or take a year off from his studies and teach abroad. He's afraid he'll make the wrong decision, so he's putting off deciding. Kenny's decision-making skills are hampered by his belief that every problem has a perfect solution and that he mustn't act until he has the perfect answer to his problem. He believes it would be a disaster if he decided to do something that he later regretted, or if it turned out that the other option would have been better.

We make decisions every day. Some are trivial, such as what to have for dinner or which movie to see. Other decisions are more important, such as choosing a career or a life partner. Ideally, you want to make the right decision. No one enjoys making decisions they later regret. But in their quest to find the right decision, many people are paralyzed by the fear of making the wrong choice and often end up taking the path of least resistance - no matter where that leads.

The idea that there's a perfect answer to every problem and decision, coupled with the idea that you *must* find the perfect solution to every problem and that it would be catastrophic if you made the wrong choice holds you back from making the most of your life.

While you dillydally, trying to make up your mind what to do, opportunities may vanish. Time may run out before you act, so you miss out on that job you were thinking of applying for, the medical condition you were considering treating becomes inoperable, or the woman of your dreams marries another man because you couldn't decide whether or not to propose to her.

Very few problems have an absolutely perfect solution. Even if a perfect answer exists, there's no reason why you must find that solution. There's no law of the universe compelling you to make absolutely correct decisions. While some choices lead to unfortunate consequences, very few of them turn out to be fatal or to lead to the end of the world. No matter how bad a choice turns out to be, you will almost certainly survive it.

We have some control over our lives, but we don't have total control. You can't be certain how things will turn out. What appears the right decision today may, because of changing circumstances, turn out to be the wrong decision tomorrow. At first, a possible solution may seem perfect but it will often turn out in ways you don't expect. From time to time, you'll choose a solution that isn't as good as you thought it would be. Since you can't predict the future, you had better accept uncertainty and the reality there is no guaranteed perfect solution to your problems.

If you insist on finding a perfect solution or making the absolutely correct choice, you'll make yourself anxious out of your fear of getting it wrong. This anxiety will make it even more difficult for you to choose a suitable solution.

Most problems have several solutions or options to choose from. Some better than others. If you keep looking for the "perfect" answer, you may lose sight of other suitable solutions. In your quest to make the perfect choice, your tunnel vision will prevent you from solving your problems.

Your quest for a perfect solution leads to self-downing. First, you tell yourself you must find the perfect solution and if you don't it means there's something wrong with you. Secondly, if the decision you make turns out to be the wrong one, you give yourself an unduly hard time over your poor decision-making. You'll be much better off if you treat decision-making as a scientific experiment whereby you try out a solution and see how well it works. If it doesn't work as well as you'd hoped, perhaps you can try a different solution.

While you're busy looking for the perfect solution to one of your problems, your other problems will mount up and remain unresolved. A much more effective approach to problems is to make a list of several possible solutions. Then, instead of looking for the perfect one, choose which you think would be the best solution from your list and try it out. See how well it works.

Decision-making in a scientific manner takes practice. The more practice you have, the better you'll get at solving your problems. If you keep looking for a perfect solution, you'll never get to try out other possible choices, and you won't get to practice and improve your problem-solving skills.

Key Point: Very few problems have perfect solutions, and when you're presented with a number of options, there is seldom an absolutely right one. The quest for a perfect solution is a fool's errand. There's no reason why you must find the perfect solution or make the absolutely right choice.

**

IDEA #12: YOU'RE ALREADY GOOD ENOUGH

Angelina has low self-esteem. She believes some people are better than others and she thinks she isn't good enough and should be better than she is. She feels better about herself when she does well on a task or gets compliments from others, but the boost to her self-esteem is only temporary. Angelina craves constant reassurance from others that she's good enough and that they like her. She believes you can tell the merit of people by their deeds and by how many friends they have. She also believes that some people are rotten to the core.

Our self-image is the way we see ourselves. We often use labels to describe our self-image: attractive, sexy, lazy, honest, resourceful, hopeless, disgusting, worthless, exceptional, outstanding, stupid, fat, hard-working, pathetic, good, bad, et cetera.

The trouble with these labels is that they are over-generalizations. They only describe a small part of us; they don't describe us in our entirety. Yet most of us foolishly use these inadequate, incomplete labels to ascertain our total worth as human beings. When we apply a positive label to ourselves, we have a temporary boost to our self-esteem. On the other hand, when we apply a negative label to ourselves, our self-esteem plummets.

While you can label your actions as good or bad, depending on the consequences and motivations, a single adjective like "good" or "bad" doesn't come close to describing something as complex as a unique, multifaceted human being. "People rating" is irrational because it assumes that people can be given a single, global rating, and then have their rating compared with the ratings of others. It implies that some people are better than others. It suggests that one aspect of us (e.g., our behavior, or our appearance) is the only thing that matters. According to people rating, if you're better looking than I am, then you're a better person than I. Or if you give more money to charity than I do, you're a better person, regardless of whatever other actions you or I might have taken in the past or might take in the future.

The idea that you can give people (including yourself) a global rating, such as good or bad, and rate one human being as "better" than another is perhaps the most dangerous idea ever uttered. Rating yourself higher than you rate others leads to grandiosity, vanity, and bigotry. Rating yourself lower than others leads to shame and depression. In short, people rating is a recipe for emotional and interpersonal disaster. Here are just some of the reasons this idea makes no sense:

Having a skill, such as being able to sing or mend broken computers, is an asset that brings many advantages. However, the skill doesn't make you a better person than someone who lacks the skill. Similarly, if you lack those skills, you're not a worse person than someone who can sing or fix computers. Being skilled at one thing (or many things) doesn't make you a good person. Nor does being incompetent at one thing (or many things) make you a bad person.

Nobody is good at everything. As noted above, the ability to fix computers might have its advantages, but if you can fix a computer but can't sing, does that make you a better person than someone who can't fix computers but who can sing? Or is the other person better than you? It's impossible to measure the worth of person based on only one trait or characteristic.

Nor is it possible to rate a person based on many of his or her traits and behaviors. We don't know everything there is to know about people. We might see someone doing a variety of good deeds (for example, saving someone from a burning building, helping out in the community, or acting kindly toward the elderly) and think they're a "good person." But what we don't know is that (for example) the same person is often cruel to small children, cheats on her husband, and steals from her employer. Therefore, the person is not as "good" as we thought.

If you do something well today but do it poorly tomorrow, are you a better person on the day when you do it well? It seems ludicrous to suggest that your worth and value as a person varies from day to day based on how well you perform certain tasks. You're still the same person whether you do a task well or do it poorly.

We all change from day to day. Some days you're polite, while on other days you may be rude. Some days you may be stressed and harried and on other days calm and resourceful. It makes no sense to suggest that on the days when you're polite and calm that you're a good person, while of the other days you're a bad person.

Key Point: You can't make yourself a better person. Nor can you make yourself a worse person. You're already good enough - a prime specimen of humanity: you're human (obviously); you're living and breathing; you make mistakes from time to time, just like humans are supposed to; you're unique, there's no one exactly like you; and you're in a constant state of change, learning and growing based on your experiences. Human beings don't come any better than that.

***

ABOUT THE AUTHOR

Will Ross taught himself how to use Rational Emotive Behavior Therapy (REBT) and now teaches other REBT self-helpers. He is the author and publisher of online REBT self-help materials and the co-founder of the REBT Network, a major online resource for REBT practitioners, their clients, and students of REBT. This is how he describes his work:

"When Albert Ellis created Rational Emotive Behavior Therapy in the 1950's, he created one of the first self-help therapies. Many people can teach themselves REBT as I did, but some people need extra help. That's what I do: I tutor people who want extra help. Over the years, I've created a number of self-help tools and written a number of articles designed to help people help themselves with REBT. I also work privately, one-on-one, with those who request it, helping them to remain focused and master the techniques and philosophy so that they can overcome their problems, reach their goals, and lead a rewarding and joyous life."

AUTHOR'S NOTE

This book is designed to provide accurate information in regard to the subject matter covered. It is distributed with the understanding that it is not a substitute for psychological, medical, or other professional services. If expert assistance or counseling is needed, the services of a competent professional should be sought.

Please help spread the word.

If you enjoyed this book and found it helpful, please leave a review at Amazon. Your review will encourage others to discover the benefits of REBT.

Gratefully,

Will Ross

Made in the USA
Las Vegas, NV
16 May 2024